25.70

W9-AAH-905

WITHDRAWN

ANDERSON PUBLIC LIBRARY
ANDERSON, INDIANA

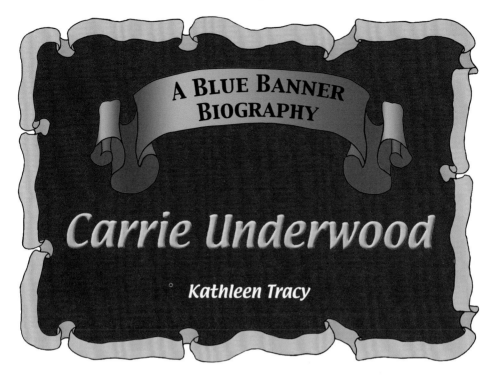

A BLUE BANNER
BIOGRAPHY

Carrie Underwood

Kathleen Tracy

Mitchell Lane
PUBLISHERS

P.O. Box 196
Hockessin, Delaware 19707
Visit us on the web: www.mitchelllane.com
Comments? email us: mitchelllane@mitchelllane.com

Mitchell Lane PUBLISHERS

Copyright © 2006 by Mitchell Lane Publishers. Updated 2008. All rights reserved. No part of this book may be reproduced without written permission from the publisher. Printed and bound in the United States of America.

Printing   4   5   6   7   8   9

Blue Banner Biographies

Akon	Alan Jackson	Alicia Keys
Allen Iverson	Ashanti	Ashlee Simpson
Ashton Kutcher	Avril Lavigne	Bernie Mac
Beyoncé	Bow Wow	Britney Spears
Carrie Underwood	Chris Brown	Chris Daughtry
Christina Aguilera	Christopher Paul Curtis	Ciara
Clay Aiken	Condoleezza Rice	Daniel Radcliffe
David Ortiz	Derek Jeter	Eminem
Eve	Fergie (Stacy Ferguson)	50 Cent
Gwen Stefani	Ice Cube	Jamie Foxx
Ja Rule	Jay-Z	Jennifer Lopez
Jessica Simpson	J. K. Rowling	Johnny Depp
JoJo	Justin Berfield	Justin Timberlake
Kate Hudson	Keith Urban	Kelly Clarkson
Kenny Chesney	Lance Armstrong	Lindsay Lohan
Mariah Carey	Mario	Mary J. Blige
Mary-Kate and Ashley Olsen	Michael Jackson	Miguel Tejada
Missy Elliott	Nancy Pelosi	Nelly
Orlando Bloom	P. Diddy	Paris Hilton
Peyton Manning	Queen Latifah	Ron Howard
Rudy Giuliani	Sally Field	Selena
Shakira	Shirley Temple	Tim McGraw
Usher	Zac Efron	

Library of Congress Cataloging-in-Publication Data
Tracy, Kathleen.
      Carrie Underwood / by Kathleen Tracy.
          p. cm. — (A blue banner biography)
      Includes bibliographical references (p.), discography (p.), and index.
      ISBN 1-58415-425-X (library bound)
      1. Underwood, Carrie, 1983 — Juvenile literature. 2. Singers — United States —
Biography — Juvenile literature. I. Title. II. Series.
ML3930.U53T73 2005
782. 421642'092 — dc22
                                               2005019489
ISBN-13: 9781584154259

ABOUT THE AUTHOR: Kathleen Tracy has been a journalist for over twenty years. Her writing has been featured in magazines including *The Toronto Star*'s "Star Week," *A&E Biography* magazine, *KidScreen* and *TV Times*. She is also the author of numerous biographies, including *William Hewlett: Pioneer of the Computer Age*, *The Fall of the Berlin Wall*, *Gwen Stefani*, *Mariah Carey*, and *Kelly Clarkson* for Mitchell Lane Publishers.

PHOTO CREDITS: Cover, p. 4 — Jamie Kondrchek; p. 7 — Ed Rode/WireImage; p. 16 Kevin Winter/Getty Images; p. 20 Ray Micksaw/WireImage; p. 25 Ray Micksaw/ Wireimage; p. 28 Jamie Kondrchek

PUBLISHER'S NOTE: The following story has been thoroughly researched, and to the best of our knowledge, represents a true story. While every possible effort has been made to ensure accuracy, the publisher will not assume liability for damages caused by inaccuracies in the data, and makes no warranty on the accuracy of the information contained herein. This story has not been authorized or endorsed by Carrie Underwood.

CONTENTS

Chapter 1
A Legendary Stage 5

Chapter 2
"Where the Wind Comes
Sweeping Down the Plains" 10

Chapter 3
Lessons Learned 14

Chapter 4
An Unexpected Opportunity 19

Chapter 5
America's New Idol 24

Chronology 30

Discography 30

For Further Reading 31

Index 32

In May 2005, Carrie Underwood became the fourth American Idol. She was the first country singer to win the competition. Born and raised in Oklahoma, Underwood will move to Nashville to record her first album.

A Legendary Stage

*F*or anybody who aspires to become a country singer, there is no greater honor than to perform on the Grand Ole Opry radio show. Broadcast from the Grand Ole Opry House auditorium in Nashville, it is the oldest-running live radio program in the world. First broadcast in 1925, the program now reaches millions of people worldwide. For Carrie Underwood, singing at the Opry was literally a dream come true.

Less than two weeks after winning the *American Idol* crown, Underwood was invited to the Country Music Association's annual festival. She was warmly greeted by the other performers and the thousands of fans who had waited for hours to meet her.

Ironically, the last time Underwood attended the CMA Music Festival was when she was a fifteen-year-old fan. She remembers standing in line for autographs. "I'm from Oklahoma and grew up listening to country music," she said in an Associated Press interview. "I think it's the most cheerful music."

> *Ironically, the last time Underwood attended the CMA Music Festival was when she was a fifteen-year-old fan.*

The 2005 Nashville festival was a whirlwind of activity for Underwood. On June 8 she participated in CMT's 100 Greatest Duets concert, performing the song "Does He Love You?" with Jamie O'Neal. Not only did the packed crowd greet her with one of the largest ovations of the night, they cheered wildly every time she hit a high note.

The following evening she performed with singer-songwriter Phil Vassar. She also sang her *American Idol* single "Inside Your Heaven." But the highlight of the week for Underwood was her appearance on the Grand Ole Opry radio show on June 10. Even though she had been performing since she was a kid, Underwood admitted to writer John Gerome that she was feeling butterflies before walking onstage. "It's such a sacred place. So many people have played there."

Underwood also told the *Tennessean* that she was a bit starstruck. "I'm lucky. It's like I have the coolest backstage pass ever. It's just been so wonderful

Carrie poses with country star Jamie O'Neal backstage at the Greatest Duets concert, held during the 2005 CMT Music Festival. Underwood and O'Neal performed Does He Love You? *Carried admitted that she was star-struck meeting so many famous singers.*

because I'm just a fan myself. And I get to be around all these people I've only heard about—and I get to stand onstage with them!"

Carrie was also overwhelmed by how welcoming everyone was. When she walked into her dressing room before the Opry show, she found two bouquets of flowers waiting for her. One was from her favorite band, Rascal Flatts. The other was from Trisha Yearwood, who was also performing at the Opry that night.

For the first time, an American Idol would record a country album—in Nashville.

For Underwood, the experience promised to be the beginning of an exciting new chapter in her life. For the first time, an American Idol would record a country album—in Nashville. "I love it here," she excitedly told writer Brad Schmitt. "Everybody's so nice. And it's the kind of music I feel at home with."

American Idol creator Simon Fuller, who also runs the record label for the show's winners, told the *Tennessean* he believes Carrie will be one of the biggest crossover stars ever. "I see a huge opportunity right now for the right country artist to break into the whole world, never mind mainstream America, but the whole world. I think the right person is Carrie. She's adorable, talented, and everyone who voted for her will be proud of the record she's going to make."

Underwood's goal is to appeal to as many people as possible. "I think there'll be two different audiences involved," she explained in a Billboard.com interview. "There'll be the country people, who are really embracing me right now and standing behind me, and I am so thankful for that. Then there are the people who don't necessarily like country music but watched the show and liked me. You wouldn't believe the people who come up and are like, *Oh, we watched the show and voted for you.* The show transcends age, gender, ethnicity, everything. Hopefully I reached a new kind of audience and opened a few people's eyes to country music."

> **"Hopefully I reached a new kind of audience and opened a few people's eyes to country music."**

While Underwood may have taken America by surprise with her bubbly personality and sparkling talent, she didn't fool those who knew her growing up. They say it was clear from an early age that Carrie was not only a special person, but a unique talent who was destined for stardom.

"Where the Wind Comes Sweeping Down the Plains"

*O*klahoma is one of the Great Plains states, which are known for farmland that is flat as far as the eye can see. Carrie Marie Underwood grew up in Checotah, Oklahoma. The town has less than 4,000 residents and is so small that it only has one traffic light. It is most famous for being the steer wrestling capital of the world. Steer wrestling is a rodeo sport in which a cowboy jumps off his horse and wrestles a steer to the ground. Whoever can do it the fastest, wins.

Carrie was born on March 10, 1983. Her mother, Carole, gave birth to Carrie at home, rather than at a hospital. Carole is a retired schoolteacher, and Steve, Carrie's father, is a retired plant worker who now raises cattle. Carrie is the youngest of three daughters.

Her older sisters, Shanna and Stephanie, are both elementary school teachers.

As a young girl growing up on the family farm in Checotah—which is about an hour's drive from Tulsa in the eastern part of the state—Carrie developed a deep love for animals. That's one of the reasons she became a vegetarian, a person who doesn't eat meat. She would become attached to the cattle on the farm and couldn't stand the thought of eating them. Carrie was also always bringing home stray animals. But her mom says Carrie loved creatures of *all* kinds.

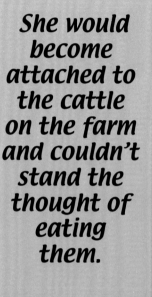

She would become attached to the cattle on the farm and couldn't stand the thought of eating them.

"You all may not know it, but in Oklahoma we have little bag worms that get on cedar trees," Carole revealed on ET.com. "I have seen her, when she was little, go out and get bag worms and put them all over her. She is just an animal person. She has had little snakes that she played with. She was a tomboy."

While some people might have been bored growing up in such a small community, Carrie loved it. "I really like the fact that I came from a small town because things are different in a small town," she explained on MSNBC.com. "When I was a little girl, I'd climb trees and catch frogs and go fishing and stuff like that." She also loved softball, which she played for eight years.

But her dream since she could remember was to be a singer. Carrie jokes that she could sing before she could talk. Her grandfather, Carl Shatswell, says it was obvious Carrie was born with natural talent and destined to become a star. "I figured she'd make something of it, because she's sung all of her life," he recalled in an Associated Press interview. "She went to Kansas one time and was singing on the bus. Her grandmother and me, we tried to get her to hush up, but the rest of the folks on there, they wanted her to keep singing. She was just three at the time."

Although Carrie was always quiet and polite, when it came to singing she was not shy about letting people know her dreams.

Although Carrie was always quiet and polite, when it came to singing she was not shy about letting people know her dreams. "If you were to ask me what I would be when I grow up when I was little I would've been like, I want to be famous," she admitted to MSNBC.com.

Sometimes, Carrie could be a little *too* into music. "When I was little, I would put on my headphones and I would rock out and sing the wrong words to every single song imaginable," she recalled to the *Muskogee Phoenix* newspaper. "My sister would get *so* mad at me."

Carrie first started singing publicly at area festivals, at the local Lion's Club, and in her church choir at the First Freewill Baptist Church. She also regularly entered talent contests and shows. Suzanne Roberts, an eighth-grade American history teacher who helped organize the annual Robin Emerson Memorial Talent Show, recalled to writer Ronn Smith that Underwood had an obvious gift—and belief in herself.

Carrie first started singing publicly at area festivals, at the local Lion's Club, and in her church choir.

"Carrie performed every year from junior high through high school," Roberts said. "When we first heard her sing, you could see the stars in her eyes. She knew when she was very young what she wanted to do and she followed that dream. We teased her in junior high that she would be famous one day. I told her I wanted concert tickets, and I'm going to hold her to that."

But Underwood would discover that the road to success wouldn't always be smooth.

CHAPTER 3

Lessons Learned

*C*arrie's parents were supportive of her dreams of becoming a singer. When she was thirteen, they paid for their daughter to travel to Nashville to record a demo CD. Carrie's dream was to become the next LeAnn Rimes, who had recorded her breakout song, "Blue," as a young teenager.

After recording the demo, Carrie tried to drum up interest in her singing by sending the demo to radio stations and record labels. Despite her high hopes, nothing came from the experience. Looking back, Underwood realizes it was a blessing in disguise.

"I honestly think it's a lot better that nothing came out of it now, because I wouldn't have been ready then," she acknowledged to *World Scene*. "Everything has a way of working out. Obviously there was a reason that that didn't happen." Carrie admits she actually has a hard time listening to the demo now. "I sound like a little kid — and I was."

Undaunted by the setback, Carrie continued to perform locally in between all her other activities. At Checotah High School, she was a cheerleader, and she played softball and basketball. When she got older she spent a summer working as a page for Oklahoma State Representative Bobby Frame. She also did volunteer work at Carter Healthcare and Hospice in Tahlequah. The center's volunteer coordinator, Lou Ann Hunter, recalls Carrie's compassion. "She sat with a terminal patient once a week," Hunter was quoted in *The Muskogee Phoenix*. "This isn't a high-profile thing to do. This person has to commit to training. It requires someone with depth of character. She always showed up."

Undaunted by the setback, Carrie continued to perform locally in between all her other activities.

Carrie's Sunday school teacher, Gina Payne, agreed. She told the *Muskogee Phoenix* one of her most vivid memories was of Underwood doing volunteer work at a battered women's shelter. "She was always behind the scenes — she was never one to grab the

Carrie, shown here at age twenty-two, says that when she was thirteen years old she traveled to Nashville to record a CD. She wanted to follow in the footsteps of then-teen sensation LeAnn Rimes. Although disappointed at the time nothing came of the recordings, Carrie now says she glad because she would not have been ready for the demands of success back then. "Things have a way of working out," she says.

limelight. She's just being who she is and not super flashy."

The teacher also remembers Underwood's quiet determination. Carrie once sent her an e-mail that Payne tacked to her refrigerator. "She was 15 or 16 and it said, *When I make it big. . . .* She knew it; she knew it."

For a while Underwood, who plays guitar and piano, performed with a five-piece band called Star Rise. Each member of the group would sing songs from a different genre, from country to pop to rock. The group traveled all over, appearing at festivals in Texas, Kansas, Missouri, Arkansas, and Tennessee. *World Scene* writer John Wooley reports that whenever kids came up and asked Carrie for an autograph, she would add a special note that said, *Follow your dreams.*

For a while Underwood, who plays guitar and piano, performed with a five-piece band called Star Rise.

Not only was Carrie a talented teen, she was also an excellent student. She was a member of the Honor Society and was class salutatorian, which means she had the second highest academic scores in her graduating class. Checotah High School Principal Pam Keeter told writer Leilani Roberts Ott that

Underwood was dedicated to learning. "She's smart, polite, respectful, quiet, never boastful, almost a little humble, never flaunted — just one of those kids."

Keeter added that Carrie was also feisty in her own way. Right before the graduation ceremony, "She was playing softball and ended up with a black eye, and maybe even a broken nose," the principal recalled to Ott. "She just came up and gave that speech and kept going. You might look at her and think she's real delicate, but she's no sissy."

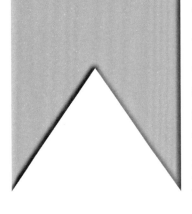

She put her dreams on hold and enrolled in college to pursue a career in broadcasting.

Even though in her heart she believed she was good enough to pursue singing as a career, after graduating from high school Underwood did some soul searching. She began to think that being a country music star simply wasn't meant for her. She put her dreams on hold and enrolled in college to pursue a career in broadcasting.

A year later FOX would premiere a new reality show called *American Idol*. And just three years later, that show would be the avenue for Underwood to dust off her childhood dreams and fulfill them beyond her wildest expectations.

An Unexpected Opportunity

*U*nderwood picked up in college where she left off in high school. She quickly earned a reputation at Northeastern State University as a bright, responsible student with a sparkling personality. She wrote for the college newspaper, *The Northeastern,* and the student online magazine *Tsa-la-gi.* She also appeared on the student-produced local access TV show *The Quah.*

Dr. Dana Eversole, the university's associate professor of mass communications, told writer Clifton Adcock that Underwood was a natural on camera. "She was funny and had cute story ideas," including segments on being a chef and adopting a pet. Eversole also recalled, "Like any other college student, she came to class in pajama pants and a ball cap."

Underwood also worked part-time as a server in a popular pizza parlor called Sam and Ella's.

Even though she was not actively pursuing a singing career, her friends at college urged her to try out for *American Idol.* "I can remember during the first or second season, we were watching the show at my apartment," sorority sister Katie Greer recounted to the *Muskogee Phoenix.* "We said, *Carrie, you should do this.* And she said, *No, Simon won't like me.*"

Underwood admits that watching the show rekindled her desire to be a professional singer. "I

Carrie initially hesitated about auditioning for American Idol *because she was afraid Simon Cowell wouldn't like her. Ironically, the often blunt-talking judge became her most vocal supporter on the show. After winning the competition Carrie posed backstage with show creator Simon Fuller (left) and Simon Cowell (right).*

kind of gave up on singing after I graduated high school," she admitted to writer Leilani Ott. "I thought, *OK, now it's time to grow up and get a real job and count that off as just a dream.* I don't know what made me want to try out for *American Idol.* All of the other seasons everybody said, *You should try out for that* and I was like, *Whatever.* But something pushed me to go and I did it."

The closest audition city was St. Louis, Missouri—an eight-hour drive from Checotah. At first, Underwood thought, *Forget it — maybe next year. That's a long way away.* But she told MSNBC.com that her mom said, "If you want to go, I'll take you." So, accompanied by her mother, Carrie joined seven thousand other hopeful contestants who converged on St. Louis.

> *The closest audition city was St. Louis, Missouri— an eight-hour drive from Checotah.*

Over the course of a week, Carrie made it through the preliminary eliminations and was among those selected to sing in front of Simon Cowell, Paula Abdul, and Randy Jackson. She chose "I Can't Make You Love Me," originally recorded by Bonnie Raitt. Out of over 100,000 participants who tried out in St. Louis and the other audition cities—Cleveland, New

Orleans, Las Vegas, Orlando, San Francisco, and Washington, D.C. — Underwood was one of 193 people who were flown to Hollywood for the competition's next phase.

> **Forced to drop out of her final semester of college, Underwood relocated to Hollywood for the last three months of the competition.**

Carrie would later say she never expected to get out of the first round. But suddenly, she was on her way to California, taking an airplane trip for the first time in her life. On the strength of her performance of Martina McBride's "Independence Day," she made the cut of 44. One song later, "Young Hearts (Run Free)," a stunned Carrie found herself in the final 12. Overnight her life became a whirlwind.

Forced to drop out of her final semester of college, Underwood relocated to Hollywood for the last three months of the competition. Although she was comfortable in her new surroundings, she got the feeling others looked at her like a fish out of water.

"They find things I talk about or what I do funny," she revealed to Clifton Adcock, a reporter from an Oklahoma newspaper. "It's like last night [at a press conference] when they asked, 'What is Checotah known for?' and I said, 'Steer wrestling.'

Everybody started laughing. Some people just don't get it, and that's the funniest thing of all—watching them react to me."

Underwood was also unique in that she considered herself a country singer. And by staying true to her roots, she established herself as the early favorite. On the March 22, 2005, show, Simon Cowell made it clear he thought she had what it took not only to win the competition, but to be a true star. "Carrie, you're not just the girl to beat, you're the person to beat. I will make a prediction, not only will you win this competition, but you will sell more records than any other previous *Idol* winner!"

Simon Cowell made it clear he thought she had what it took not only to win the competition, but to be a true star.

The downside for Underwood was that she missed her family—and her pets. "The only other time I've been away from home was when I went to college," she told Katy Kroll. "And that was just an hour away, so I could always go home if I needed to. But I talk to [my family] every night."

Despite her homesickness, Carrie felt blessed. She told *World Scene*, "This is the highlight of my life so far."

Actually, the best was yet to come.

America's New Idol

*O*n May 25, 2005, Carrie Underwood was named the fourth *American Idol*, narrowly beating out rocker Bo Bice. Over 37 million votes were cast to determine the winner. Backstage after the show, Underwood recalled her thoughts the moment her name was announced. "It took me a while to realize he actually did just call my name. There were so many emotions going through me—I was nervous, I was excited. I was scared. It's going to take a couple of weeks. It hasn't hit me at all."

For winning the competition, Underwood earned a guaranteed $1 million recording contract with Arista Records, plus unlimited use of a private jet for a year. Both she and Bice were surprised with new Mustang convertibles as well. Bice was also offered a recording contract as runner-up, and Underwood went out of her way to show her support. "Once it came down to me and Bo, we both decided no matter what happened we'd both be set and we'd both be

After 37 million votes, Carrie Underwood was named the fourth American Idol *over runner-up Bo Bice. Both singers won recording contracts. They were also surprised with brand new red Mustangs.*

really happy. He's such a wonderful person. We both knew [the final vote] would be close, but I know he will do just as well, if not better, than me," she commented to Katy Kroll.

Carrie couldn't stress how, win or lose, being on *American Idol* could be the most important stepping stone for any performer. "There was never anything negative about it. It was a wonderful experience. I got to meet some of the best people I've ever met, and we all grew as people and as entertainers. Now we're looking forward to the [*American Idol*] tour."

> *From the moment her name was announced as the new Idol, Carrie found herself in the eye of a media storm.*

From the moment her name was announced as the new Idol, Carrie found herself in the eye of a media storm. It seemed everybody wanted to hear from America's new sweetheart. On the *Ellen DeGeneres Show* Underwood still seemed dazed about how winning the title would change her life. "The world is in front of me now. . . . My dreams are no longer dreams and they all have the possibility of coming true. I'm gonna get to work with some awesome people. Everything I've ever wanted to happen is happening."

But Underwood is very aware of the responsibility that comes with her sudden celebrity. She knows she is now a role model for millions of young girls across the country. "It's not so much what I say as what I do," Carrie pointed out to the *Muskogee Phoenix*. "I always swore to myself I'd never do anything that when I'm old and I have grandchildren I don't want to look back on my life and be ashamed of the things that I did. I really hope to positively influence people. We all have our idols, and there's people I look up to that never let me down and really changed my life. I don't take it lightly at all."

Underwood is aware of the responsibility that comes with her celebrity. She knows she is now a role model for girls.

Carrie's first single, "Inside Your Heaven," was released June 14. It made chart history when it broke in at number one on Billboard's Hot 100. Her album is scheduled for a fall 2005 release. One thing Underwood promises: "I'm definitely going to stick to country, maybe some crossover, like Shania and Faith Hill. That's where my heart is."

Although Underwood fully intends to finish the required three credit hours she needs to complete her college degree, it probably won't be on campus. Instead, because of her recording schedule, she will take correspondence or online classes to earn her diploma.

For the time being, Underwood will probably be splitting her time between Los Angeles and Nashville, but she is adamant that Oklahoma will always be her

Though she finds cities like Los Angeles and Nashville to be exciting, Carrie says she'll always consider Checotah home. No matter how successful she gets, Underwood plans to eventually settle down in Oklahoma. "That's where I want to raise my kids."

home. "That's where I want to end up, in a town like mine," she told the *Associated Press*. "All the people are so supportive and I never realized how much I loved that place until I was gone. Someday, when I get married, that's where I want to raise my kids."

While Underwood hopes to have a long, successful career, she told *Billboard*.com that she hopes people never lose sight of the grateful person behind the performer. "I want people to think of me as a nice person. I really am so blessed. All of this has been a great experience and I thank the American public so much for putting me in this position. I appreciate every second of it."

> *"All of this has been a great experience and I thank the American public so much for putting me in this position."*

CHRONOLOGY

1983	Born March 10 in Checotah, Oklahoma
1986	Begins singing at church
1997	Records first CD in Nashville
2001	Releases *Carrie Underwood* CD; enrolls in Northeastern State University
2002	Releases second CD: *Carrie Underwood – Live From Little Rock*; first runner-up and Talent Winner Miss NSU Scholarship Pageant
2003	Elected secretary of her sorority, Sigma Sigma Sigma
2004	Goes to St. Louis to audition for American Idol
2005	Wins American Idol; with "Inside Your Heaven," she becomes first country singer ever to break in at #1 on Billboard's Hot 100; records album, *Some Hearts*, which will become the best-selling female country album of 2005, 2006, and 2007
2006	Earns B.A., graduating magna cum laude in May; performs in over 150 shows, including tours with Kenny Chesney and Brad Paisley and a USO Tour in Kuwait and Iraq
2007	Wins two Grammys for 2006: Best New Artist and Best Female Country Vocal Performance for "Jesus, Take the Wheel"; second album, *Carnival Ride*, hits No. 1; is named Favorite Female Artist at the American Music Awards, and *Carnival Ride* is favorite country music album; "Before He Cheats" spends 64 weeks on the Billboard Hot 100, earning the longest chart run of any Hot 100 single this decade; celebrates her fifth No. 1 single, "So Small"; is *Billboard*'s Top-Selling Female Artist of 2007; is nominated for four Grammys
2008	With Keith Urban, begins Love, Pain and the Whole Crazy Carnival Ride tour

DISCOGRAPHY

1997	*The First Studio Sessions*
2001	*Carrie Underwood*
2002	*Carrie Underwood – Live From Little Rock*
2005	*Some Hearts*
2007	*Carnival Ride*

FOR FURTHER READING

While no other books are available about Carrie Underwood you might enjoy the following:

Books

Cowel, Simon. *I Don't Mean to Be Rude, But... : Backstage Gossip from American Idol & the Secrets that Can Make You a Star.* Broadway. New York: Broadway Books, 2003.

Torres, John. *Clay Aiken*. Newark, Delaware: Mitchell Lane Publishers, 2004

Tracy, Kathleen. *Clay Aiken: From Second Place to the Top of the Charts.* Newark, Delaware: Mitchell Lane Publishers, 2004.

Wheeler, Jill C. *Kelly Clarkson*. Edina, Minnesota: Checkerboard Books, 2003.

Magazines

People, March 28, 2005 issue

On the Internet

The Muskogee Phoenix
    http://www.muskogeephoenix.com

FOX
    http://www.idolonfox.com

Billboard
    http://www.billboard.com

TV Guide Online
    http://www.tvguide.com

Tulsa World
    http://www.tulsaworld.com

Grand Ole Opry
    http://www.opry.com

INDEX

Abdul, Paula   21

American Idol   18

    Audition cities   21-22

Arista Records   24

Bice, Bo   24

Blue   14

Checotah High School   15

CMA Music Festival   6

Cowell, Simon   21, 23

Does He Love You?   6

First Freewill Baptist Church
    13

Frame, Bobby   15

Fuller, Simon   8

Grand Ole Opry   5

I Can't Make You Love Me   21

Independence Day   22

Inside Your Heaven   6, 27

Jackson, Randy   21

McBride, Martina   22

Missouri, St. Louis   21

Northeaster, The   19

Northeastern State University
    19

Oklahoma, Checotah   10

O'Neal, Jamie   6

Quah, The   19

Raitt, Bonnie   21

Rascal Flatts   8

Rimes, LeAnn   14

Shatswell, Carl   12

Star Rise   17

Steer wrestling   10, 22

Tsa-la-gi   19

Underwood, Carrie

    Class Salutatorian   17

    Home town   10

    First CDs   14

    Grandfather   12

    Homesickness   23

    Honor Society   17

    Love of animals   11

    Musical instruments   17

    Parents   10

    Performing at the Opry   6

    Sisters   11

    Softball   12

    Sports   15

Volunteer work   15

Vasser, Phil   6

Yearwood, Trisha   8

Young Hearts (Run Free)   22